World of Bugs

REPULSIVE ROACHES

By Greg Roza

Gareth Stevens
Publishing

Please visit our Web site, www.garethstevens.com. For a free color catalog of all our high-quality books, call toll free 1-800-542-2595 or fax 1-877-542-2596.

Library of Congress Cataloging-in-Publication Data

Roza, Greg.
 Repulsive roaches / Greg Roza.
   p. cm. — (World of bugs)
  ISBN 978-1-4339-4608-0 (pbk.)
  ISBN 978-1-4339-4609-7 (6-pack)
  ISBN 978-1-4339-4607-3 (library binding)
 1. Cockroaches—Juvenile literature. I. Title.
 QL505.5.R69 2011
 595.7′28—dc22

                              2010031816

First Edition

Published in 2011 by
Gareth Stevens Publishing
111 East 14th Street, Suite 349
New York, NY 10003

Copyright © 2011 Gareth Stevens Publishing

Editor: Greg Roza
Designer: Christopher Logan

Photo credits: Cover, pp. 7, 9, 13, 21, 24 (feeler, wing) Shutterstock.com; pp. 1, 11, 24 (leg) iStockphoto/Thinkstock; pp. 3, 5 Hemera/Thinkstock; pp. 15, 17, 19, 24 (sack) Bates Littlehales/National Geographic/Getty Images; p. 23 Bradley Kanaris/Getty Images.

Printed in the United States of America

CPSIA compliance information: Batch #CW11GS: For further information contact Gareth Stevens, New York, New York at 1-800-542-2595.

REPULSIVE ROACHES

Most roaches are wide and long.

Some roaches are as long as your finger!

Roaches have two feelers.

9

Roaches have six legs.

11

Most roaches have wings.

13

Most roaches do not fly well.

Roach eggs grow in
a sack.

Baby roaches come out of the sack.

Most roaches hide during the day.

21

Some people race roaches!

Words to Know

feeler

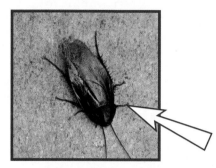

leg

sack

wing